ENGINEERING FOR DISASTER

ENGINEERING FOR AVALANCHES AND LANDSLIDES

by Samantha S. Bell

FOCUS READERS

NAVIGATOR

WWW.FOCUSREADERS.COM

Focus Readers is distributed by North Star Editions:
sales@northstareditions.com | 888-417-0195

Produced for Focus Readers by Red Line Editorial.

Content Consultant: Tong Qiu, Associate Professor of Civil Engineering, Pennsylvania State University

Photographs ©: Shutterstock Images, cover, 1, 4–5, 7, 13, 15, 16–17, 19, 20–21, 25 (top right); iStockphoto, 8–9, 26–27; Red Line Editorial, 10; Shamil Zhumatov/Reuters/Newscom, 23; Gianfranco Coscarerlia/Alamy, 25 (top left); Wally Bauman Photography/Stockimo/Alamy, 25 (bottom left); Michael Szönyi/imageBroker/Alamy, 25 (bottom right); Heather Rousseau/The Roanoke Times/AP Images, 29

Library of Congress Cataloging-in-Publication Data
Names: Bell, Samantha, author.
Title: Engineering for avalanches and landslides / by Samantha S. Bell.
Description: Lake Elmo, MN : Focus Readers, [2021] | Series: Engineering for disaster | Includes index. | Audience: Grades 4-6.
Identifiers: LCCN 2019058974 (print) | LCCN 2019058975 (ebook) | ISBN 9781644933770 (hardcover) | ISBN 9781644934531 (paperback) | ISBN 9781644936054 (pdf) | ISBN 9781644935293 (ebook)
Subjects: LCSH: Avalanches--Control--Juvenile literature. | Soil stabilization--Juvenile literature.
Classification: LCC TA714 .B45 2021 (print) | LCC TA714 (ebook) | DDC 624.1/51363--dc23
LC record available at https://lccn.loc.gov/2019058974
LC ebook record available at https://lccn.loc.gov/2019058975

Printed in the United States of America
Mankato, MN
082020

ABOUT THE AUTHOR

Samantha Bell lives with her family and lots of pets in the foothills of the Blue Ridge Mountains. She is the author of more than 100 nonfiction books for students.

TABLE OF CONTENTS

CHAPTER 1

LOST IN MUD

Oso, Washington, is a small town near the Stillaguamish River. The river runs through a valley. The surrounding hills have a history of landslides. These landslides typically begin in the hills and end at the riverbank. Over the years, the state has tried different ways to protect the valley.

Landslides can block the Stillaguamish River and cause major flooding.

In 1962, the state built a rock barrier to protect the riverbank. But in 1967, a mudslide destroyed the barrier. Another huge slide occurred in 2006. So, workers built a 1,300-foot (400-m) wall of logs. The wall was meant to keep mud from filling and blocking the river. Workers anchored the wall with 9,000-pound (4,000-kg) concrete blocks.

In 2014, heavy rains made the ground unstable. On March 22, the same hillside collapsed. The log wall was no match for the slide. Mud rushed into the valley. It covered approximately 1 square mile (2.6 sq km). In some places, the **debris** reached 80 feet (24 m) deep.

The 2014 landslide left a huge scar in the hill near Oso.

Mud blocked the flow of the river. It buried a major highway. It also crushed cars and destroyed homes. Forty-three people lost their lives.

Geologists believed the hillside was likely to slide again. They continued working with engineers. They wanted to find ways to keep people safe.

CHAPTER 2

LANDSLIDES

Landslides happen when **gravity** pulls soil and rocks downhill. Mountains and hills usually resist the pull of gravity due to the strength of soil and rocks. The roots of trees and other **vegetation** also help hold the soil and rock together. But sometimes conditions cause part of the land to slide.

The debris from landslides can block roads.

For example, **droughts** and wildfires can destroy the plants on a slope. The slope becomes less able to resist gravity. Then rain or melting snow can make the slope heavy. The pull of gravity increases. And the slope collapses.

HOW WILDFIRES CONTRIBUTE TO LANDSLIDES

1. Burning plants produce chemicals that enter the soil.

2. These chemicals create a layer in the soil that is water-resistant.

3. Water can't sink below that layer. Water collects in the soil above.

4. The water makes the soil heavy and more likely to experience landslides.

Engineers work to prevent landslides caused by too much water. They try to make the land more stable. For example, they might replant vegetation after a wildfire. Sometimes they remove rocks or soil from a hill's surface. This way, the surface won't be as steep or heavy. Engineers might also create drainage systems. The extra water flows to the base of the hill through ditches and pipes instead of into the soil.

Vibrations that shake the ground can also cause landslides. Some vibrations are natural. For example, earthquakes and volcanic eruptions create vibrations. But some vibrations are human-made.

Construction that involves drilling can shake the ground. Road traffic can, too.

Before people build on or near a slope, engineers check the land. They look for things that might cause the slope to slide someday. Sometimes they try to make the slope stronger. Plastic nets can help hold the soil in place. Debris basins can

GROWING BARRIERS

Vetiver is a type of tropical grass. It is stiff and grows quickly. Its long roots go deep into the soil. In many countries, the grass is an inexpensive way to help prevent landslides. People plant it in rows along hills. The grass holds the soil together. When landslides happen, the grass catches the debris.

Concrete barriers can help support the hillside and prevent landslides.

catch falling rocks and soil. **Retaining walls** and fences may block a slide once it starts. For example, workers built a retaining fence to protect a valley in Scotland. In October 2014, a massive landslide occurred. The fence held back more than 1,300 tons (1,180 metric tons) of soil and rock.

A NATURAL SOLUTION

Engineers know that plants can help prevent landslides. Plant roots help hold the soil together. Plants also slow the flow of water and debris.

Officials in India have used plants to prevent landslides for many years. In 1981, a conservation group started a planting program. Workers focused on 21 areas near a large mountain range. These areas had frequent landslides. Workers chose **native** plants that could grow in harsh conditions.

Workers planted in three phases. After a landslide, workers planted grasses. Next, they planted **cuttings** from shrubs and trees. Then, they planted full-grown shrubs and trees.

People can plant vetiver to help prevent landslides.

The plants grew well. They held the soil together. Within eight years, 17 of the 21 landslide areas were under control. Officials no longer considered those areas to be at risk of landslides.

CHAPTER 3

ROCKFALLS

Rockfalls happen when rocks come loose and fall from mountains or cliffs. Rocks can come loose for many reasons. Tree roots can force the rock apart. Sometimes water seeps into cracks in the rocks. If the water freezes, it expands. This expansion causes the cracks to grow.

Rocks in a rockfall can range in size from small pieces of gravel to huge boulders.

Eventually a big rock breaks into smaller pieces.

Engineers work to prevent rockfalls. Workers might drill long metal bolts into rocks. The bolts connect unstable rocks on the surface to stable rocks deep in the mountain.

OUT OF HARM'S WAY

Many people visit Yosemite National Park. In this park, rocks fall from the cliffs every 10 days on average. A geologist and an engineer worked to make the park safer. Together, they studied the dates and locations of past rockfalls. They created a map on the computer. The map helped them predict where rockfalls would happen. Workers moved cabins and other buildings to safer places.

Steel nets can help prevent rockfalls from causing harm.

Engineers also use slope drapes. These strong steel nets cover the slope. The nets control where falling rocks go. The nets stop the rocks. Or they direct the rocks into an area where the rocks won't cause damage.

CHAPTER 4

AVALANCHES

An avalanche is a huge mass of snow and ice that falls down a mountain. It buries or destroys everything in its path. Heavy snowfall causes some avalanches. The snow may pile up in unstable areas. When the snow becomes too heavy, an avalanche happens. Vibrations or movements also can cause avalanches.

Avalanches can happen without warning and cause major destruction.

Engineers work to reduce the risk of avalanches. They build wooden or metal fences. Some fences slow down the wind. Others collect drifting snow. Engineers may even deliberately cause an avalanche. They look for slopes covered by heavy snow. They place explosives along the slope. The explosives go off. The resulting avalanche is controlled. The slope becomes stable and safe again.

Engineers might replant forests. Trees can slow down or block the falling snow. Sometimes engineers design concrete snowsheds. These structures are built over roads. They act like tunnels during avalanches. Engineers also design

An expert starts a controlled avalanche to prevent unexpected avalanches that could hurt people.

wedge-shaped walls to protect buildings. The wedge shape directs the snow to either side. It reduces the force of the avalanche. It keeps the snow from hitting buildings straight on.

Deflecting dams also change the direction of an avalanche. For example, in 1995, an avalanche hit the village of Flateyri, Iceland. Twenty people lost their lives. After the disaster, workers built two deflecting dams above the village. More avalanches hit in 1999 and 2000.

TESTING AVALANCHES IN NORWAY

The Ryggfonn test site opened in Norway in 1981. Engineers create avalanches at the site. They then study the avalanches. They see how much snow falls. They record how fast it moves. And they measure how far the snow reaches. Then, they design structures to help stop the avalanches. They test these structures to see how well they work.

Both times, the dams sent the snow into the ocean. The dams kept the village safe from the avalanches.

AVALANCHE PROTECTION

DEFLECTING DAMS

direct avalanches toward areas where they will cause less harm

SNOW FENCES

slow down wind and collect drifting snow

SNOWSHEDS

cover roadways to protect vehicles passing through

WEDGE-SHAPED WALLS

direct snow away from buildings or other structures

CHAPTER 5

PROTECTING THE FUTURE

Climate change is a human-caused crisis. It involves long-term changes in Earth's weather patterns. As a result of these changes, extreme weather conditions are becoming more common. These conditions include heavy rainfall and snowfall. They also include wildfires.

Wildfires can make the land more likely to slide.

All of these conditions increase the risk of landslides and avalanches.

Engineers want people to know whether an area is safe. So, they work to identify places that are at risk. A technology called lidar helps them. Lidar stands for Light Detection and Ranging. Lidar sends laser pulses through the vegetation of an area. Engineers use the data to create a model of the land's surface. They can learn how the land formed. They can study the history of landslides in the area. And they can accurately map new landslides. With this information, engineers can better predict what the land will do in the future.

An expert uses a lidar tool to study the features of the land.

Many factors can put an area at risk of landslides or avalanches. The shape of the land is important. The type and amount of vegetation makes a difference. The amount of snow or rainfall has big effects, too. Engineers use all of this information. They work hard to help keep people safe.

FOCUS ON
ENGINEERING FOR AVALANCHES AND LANDSLIDES

Write your answers on a separate piece of paper.

1. Write a letter to a friend describing what you learned about the causes of landslides.

2. Do you think people should be allowed to do activities in areas at risk of avalanches? Why or why not?

3. Which structure is used to catch rocks and soil from landslides?
   - **A.** deflecting dam
   - **B.** debris basin
   - **C.** retaining wall

4. Ice contributes to rockfalls by doing what?
   - **A.** creating an icy slope for rocks to slide down
   - **B.** preventing plants from growing on the slope
   - **C.** expanding cracks in rocks and causing the rocks to come loose

Answer key on page 32.

GLOSSARY

cuttings
Pieces cut from plants that are used to grow new plants.

debris
The remains of something broken.

droughts
Long periods of little or no rain.

geologists
Scientists who study Earth's crust.

gravity
The natural force that pulls objects toward Earth.

native
Living or growing naturally in a particular region.

retaining walls
Walls that hold back soil.

vegetation
All of the plants found in a certain area.

TO LEARN MORE

BOOKS

Hudak, Heather C. *Landslide and Avalanche Readiness.* New York: Crabtree Publishing, 2020.

Otfinoski, Steven. *Avalanches.* New York: Scholastic, 2016.

Owings, Lisa. *What Protects Us During Natural Disasters?* Minneapolis: Lerner Publications, 2016.

NOTE TO EDUCATORS

Visit **www.focusreaders.com** to find lesson plans, activities, links, and other resources related to this title.

INDEX

Answer Key: **1.** Answers will vary; **2.** Answers will vary; **3.** B; **4.** C